The Art

of

Joyful Aging

Joanne Turney Bauers

Edgewood Publishing Company
4000 Cathedral Avenue, Suite 628 B
Washington, DC 20016

ISBN 978-0-9660611-5-4

Library of Congress Control Number 2008940770

Printed in China

DISCLAIMER

This book contains useful information concerning the subject matter.

Some affirmations were expressed by famous people and taken from various
publications with credit given to the writer. Others were provided by relatives
and friends, some of whom did not wish to be identified.

The contents of this publication should not be construed as professional advice and
neither the publisher nor the author is engaged in rendering advice in this category.
If professional assistance is required, the services of a competent professional should
be sought.

INTRODUCTION

I first became acquainted with Joanne Turney and her art work in 1990. She was having an exhibition in a Soho New York gallery and I was editor in chief of Manhattan Arts International magazine. Upon meeting her I was immediately impressed by the vitality, positive energy and generosity of spirit that radiated from her and her paintings.

Today at the ripe young age of 79, Joanne's gusto is as powerful as ever in this unique and inspiring book *"The Art of Joyful Aging"* - a direct reflection of her *joie de vivre*.

Most of Joanne's paintings are large, however, the paintings that are reproduced within are her "Teeny Turneys." Although small in scale these precious gems encompass an enormous magnitude of versatility, expressive colors, and rich textures. Her luminous abstract paintings are a celebration of the internal rhythms of the natural world and the creative gifts from the metaphysical realm.

To accompany her paintings Joanne has thoughtfully gathered and placed a variety of quotes about aging that range from witty humor to profound insight. This poetic companion of art and words guides the reader on a blissful journey through the ever changing seasons of life.

As a curator I have selected Joanne's paintings for several New York City exhibitions and have observed how viewers stand in awe of her artistic prowess. Joanne, however, is always quick to dismiss flattery. Instead, she acknowledges she is the vessel through which the Creator expresses itself. Only someone like Joanne, with humility and grace, could create such a treasure trove to honor humanity. Her faith has been always a constant flame burning brightly within her and emanating from her creations, and this incredible book is no exception.

We can learn from Joanne who has mastered the art of living in the present and celebrates life with daily gratitude and reverence. She views aging as an opportunity for growth and transformation and her spiritual philosophy is clear.

Renée Phillips,
New York based author, public speaker,
and Director, Manhattan Arts International

ACKNOWLEDGEMENTS

I want to thank my husband and friends

for their loyal support and positive affirmations.

Without them this book would not have been possible.

Credits:
Joanne Turney Bauers - *Original art*
Jelko Yuresha - *Cover photography and contributions*
Tom Owen - *Layout, production and cover design*

DEDICATION

This book is dedicated to humanity.

Its purpose is to emphasize the importance of aging

And the many values that we receive

As all of us share this journey.

THE BEAUTY OF AGING

No doubt, people think differently about aging around the world. In third world countries and other countries, not as advanced as America, people think more of survival, where their next meal will come from, and whether there is clean water to drink. In these countries, people do not think of aging, but of survival.

In America, when we are young and entering the "springtime of our lives", we never consider aging. Nevertheless, we look forward to growing older, more mature, more knowledgeable, and becoming equals with our parents. When we begin to enter the work force, we think of opportunities, wealth generation, and how we may achieve financial independence for our later years. But as we go through "the summer of our lives", with all its trials and tribulations, we continue to try to achieve our aspirations. During this process, we become more mature, wiser, and aware of the needs of our fellow man.

But as we approach the "autumn of our lives", we begin to think of our vulnerabilities and how age may be catching up to us. We start slowing down, begin to see wrinkles, and feel like our youth is behind us. But this is not a bad thing!

The knowledge, experience, and trials and tribulations we have encountered, have made us stronger, better, wiser, and more valuable to our families, friends, and most of all, our country. As we approach the "winter of our years", we will know that the knowledge and wisdom we have accumulated can be shared with others, and this is where the true beauty of aging begins. We can extend a hand, wisdom, literacy, humanity, and share our efforts with others.

Thus, in America, the beauty of aging allows our minds to see the world through a different prism, a wider lens, and address family, friendship, and life's challenges with a more thoughtful perspective. In this regard, we can leave this world better than when we entered it. This is the true beauty of aging.

Susan & Raymond Petniunas

The Author

The character of a country

can be seen simply in how

it treats its old people

Bratzlover
1770 - 1811

FOREWARD

With the words and affirmations chosen by Joanne Turney you can balance your life from "inside out," rather than from "outside in." You need this book to maintain a youthful attitude. Turney's faith is infinitely more powerful than any commercials proclaiming the Fountain of Youth. When I met Joanne many years ago, my life and my career – everything, was at an end. It was her constant prayer and encouragement that changed my thinking and consequently my life.

Thank you, Joanne, for making this world a better place with this wonderful publication, and for your unwavering faith. You are living proof – *"The Art of Joyful Aging"* is there for us to have if we believe; this book provides life giving medicine without unwelcome side effects. The words Joanne Turney chose are not just words – they are a very potent wisdom of different generations illuminating our path to enjoyment and respect for the aging.

This book is not only for the wise and the old but for the benefit of any generation choosing to prepare for the aging process and its joys. Turney's faith has helped to change my life – so I believe it also could change yours.

Jelko Yuresha
British Artist, ABT Producer,
Author, Photographer

To Sho Sho
Nicholes and Anne
all my good thoughts
Sincerely.
Delko Yuresha
NYC. 25 V. 2011

Age is an opportunity no less than youth itself

Though in another dress,

And as the evening twilight fades away,

The sky is filled with stars invisible by day.

Henry Wadsworth Longfellow
1807 - 1882

Spring

Everyone believes in their youth

That the world really began with them

And everything exists for their sake.

Goethe
1749 - 1832

Life Experience

Like fine wine and cheese

We don't get older

We get better.

Anonymous

Spirituality

My age is none of my business.

Do not regret growing older,

It is a privilege denied many.

If I don't notice age, it won't notice me.

"The Group"

Attitude

As we grow older

The beauty grows inward.

Bronson Alcott
1799-1888

Inner Beauty

You are as young as your faith

As old as your doubts

As young as your self confidence

As old as your fear

As young as your hope

As old as your despair.

General Douglas MacArthur

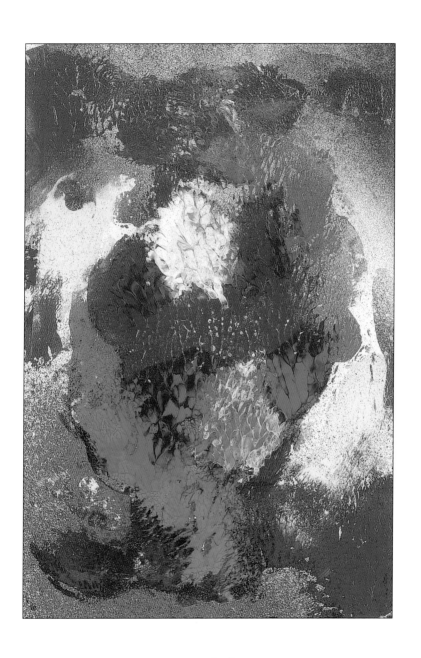

Faith

Finding the positiveness

In each of us as we age

Makes life like a great garden

Filled with blooming flowers

In beautiful array.

Jelko Yuresha

The Garden

The older I get the greater power I seem to have

To help the world.

I am like a snowball.

The further I am rolled the more I gain.

Susan B. Anthony

Power

A sense of humor

Is the best gift for aging.

Joanne Turney Bauers

The Beauty of Laughter

It is a joy to wake up in the morning,

To read the obituary

And find your name

Is not there.

Unknown

Morning

Ageism is any discrimination against people

On the basis of chronological age

Whether old or young.

It is responsible for an enormous neglect

Of social resources.

Margie Kuhn
1905-1995

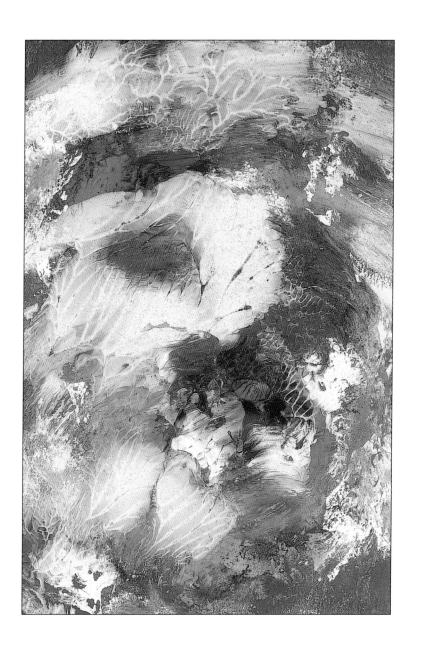

Responsibility

Age is mind over matter.

If you don't mind, it doesn't matter.

Leroy "Satchel" Paige

Reason

When we are young we are courageous.

It is only with age that prudence is

At its height.

Bion
325-255 B.C.

Prudence

To me old age is always

15 years older than I am.

Bernard M. Baruch
1859-1965

Spring

Reality

It's more scary growing up than getting older,

And even though, that doesn't mean you

Always have to act your age.

Alyson Hills Martin
Age 19

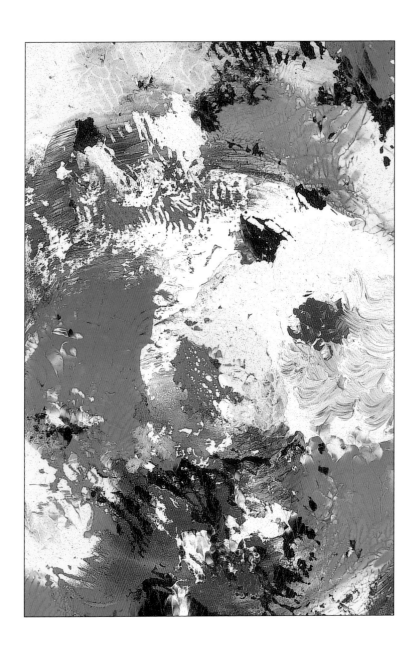

Youth

The good thing about aging

Is being comfortable

With knowing myself and my limits.

Also being able to say - "No more."

C. Loran Hills

Contentment

Grow old along with me the best is yet to be,

The last of life for which the first was made.

Our times are in His hands.

Robert Browning

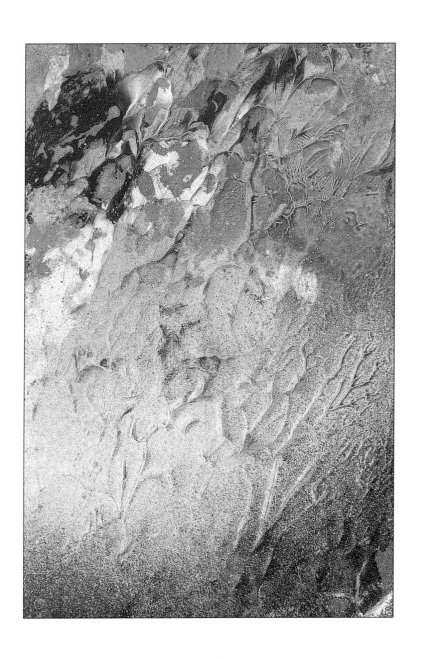

Experience

Old age takes away from us

What we have inherited

And gives us what we have earned.

Gerald Brenen
1894-1987

Wisdom

Enjoy life!

It is ungrateful not to.

Ronald Reagan

Spring

Gratitude

With age comes a better perspective

Of what is important and what is not.

You don't sweat the small stuff

For the big stuff has

More acceptable solutions.

Dr. George McCarthy

Perspective

It is nice to be here.

When you're 99 years old

It's nice to be anywhere.

George Burns
1896-1996

Summer

Put your life in God's hand

And God will guide you

Every step of the way.

Grace Hills

Honesty

Aging could be positive

Because you learn more through time.

You also have a lot more experience with life.

I think the older we get

The more we appreciate

The things we didn't know before.

Youth doesn't make choices

That are well thought out and planned

As we do with age and experience.

Amber Hills Martin
Age 17

Intelligence

I never worry about my second childhood

Because I refuse to leave my first.

Peggy Donovan

Freedom

The benefits of aging are that I am evolving

Into a more loving, joyful, light-filled person.

I am freer, wiser and healthier with each day

And filled with gratitude

For the gift of the present.

Renée Phillips

Summer

The Light

The future belongs to those who believe in

The beauty of their dreams.

Eleanor Roosevelt

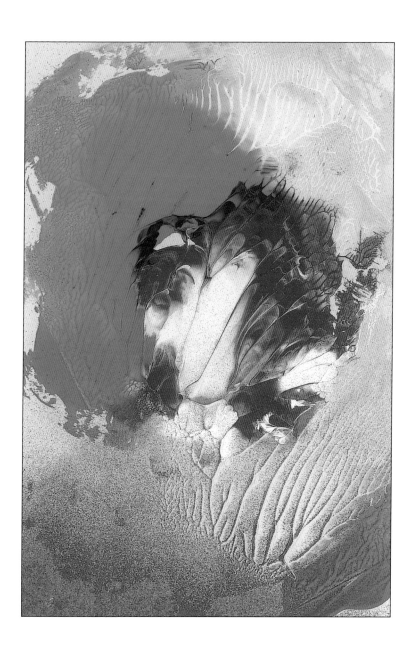

The Future

For those aging, every exit

Is an entrance

To something better.

Catherine Little

Truth

Each of us has the power to decide whether

Or not our own aging is a positive venture.

Dave Kachel

Memories

Progressive accomplishment is better than

Postponed perfection.

Pat Johnson

Summer

Perfection

With age I have learned that

The past is history,

The future is mystery

And the moment is a gift.

That is why the moment

Is called, "The Present."

Unknown

The Present

Man's mind stretched to a new idea,

Never goes back to its original dimensions.

Oliver Wendell Holmes

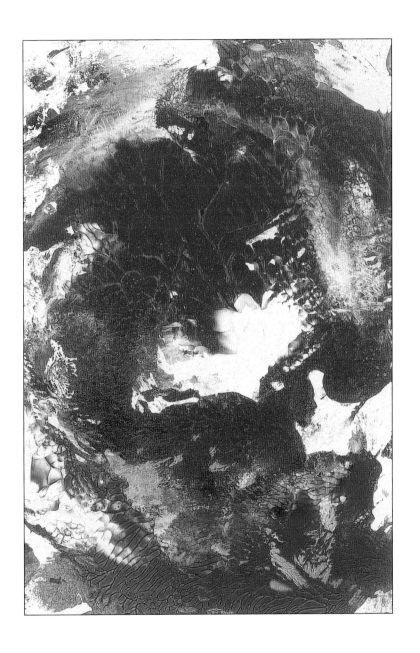

Joyful Aging

With aging comes the knowledge

Of how much I love my friends

And I am thankful

That I can be there for them.

Judy McCarthy

Summer

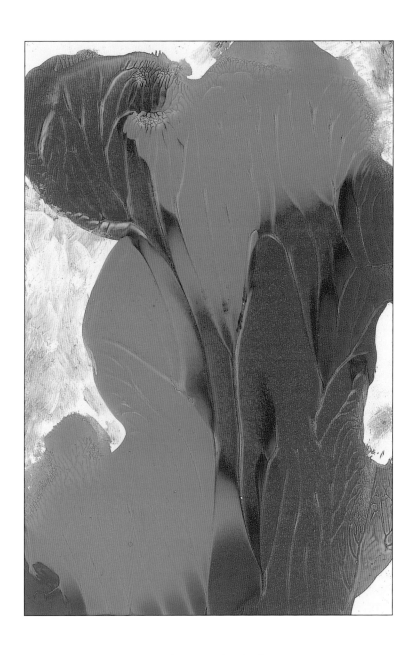

Friendship

Inside every older person

Is a younger person wondering,

"What the hell happened?"

Cora Harvey Armstrong

Enlightenment

If only I may grow firmer, simpler,

Quieter, warmer.

Dag Hammarskjold

Honor

To affect the quality of a day is

The highest art.

Henry David Thoreau

The Process

All beautiful things

Belong to the same day.

Oscar Wilde

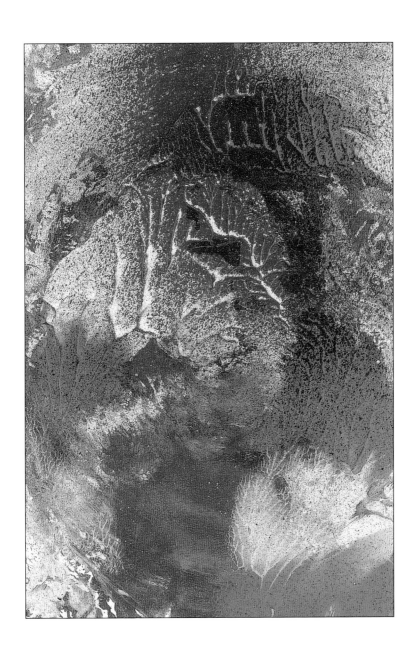

Beauty

Nothing is more beautiful than

Cheerfulness on an old face.

Jean Paul Richter

Cheerfulness

The best things in life are free

And freely offered to you and to me

So enjoy love, the Sun, the Star

For God is with you wherever you are.

F. William Bauers, Jr.

Happiness

It has taken 79 years for me

To finally realize that

Age is a gift to be treasured and enjoyed.

The Author

Realization

A new broom sweeps clean and an old

Broom knows the corners.

English Saying

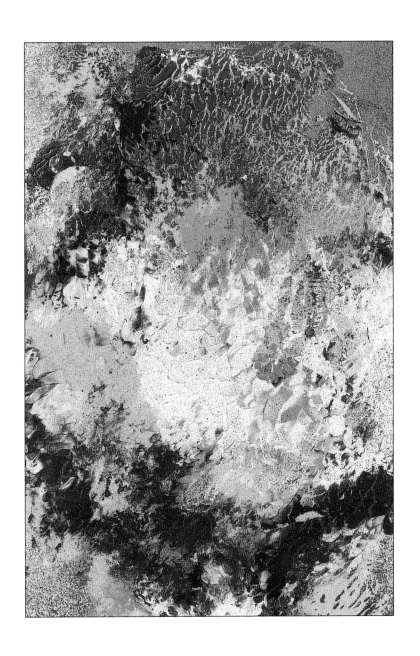

Knowledge

There are those who think — "If only_ _ _"

Who wind up sad and lonely

So decide how your life should be

Visualize, affirm, live it 'till eternity'.

Anonymous

Fall

I am an artist at living and

My work of art is my life.

Suzuke

Spirituality

It is a joy to age and actually feel your life

Is interrelated with the universe...

To feel and realize you are part and one with it

And with all mankind.

Susan Leach Hansen

Recognition

With age comes the comfort

You feel from understanding

That you are perfect

Just the way you are.

Joni Currier

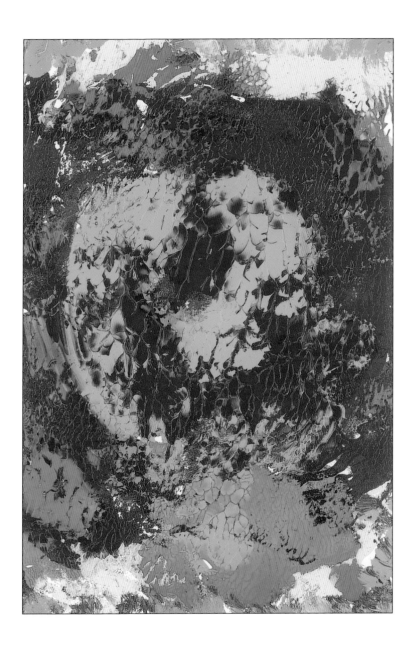

Growth

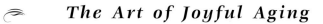

With age you get to do more grown up things

And have more freedom.

Ansley Adkins
age 8 years

F a l l

Maturity

It is the quality of life that counts

And not the number of years we live.

Elisabeth Kubler Rose

The Journey

At 70 I have accomplished all my goals

And more.

The rest of life is a gravy train.

Shirley Allison

Achievement

It is never too late to be

What you might have been.

Marjorie Turner

Hopeful

Age is a uniting factor

That we all share

So let's join hands and

Enjoy the journey together.

Elizabeth Seaman

Secure

If people are surprised when they know

My real age, it is because I am still

Very immature.

Charlotte Wiggers

Immaturity

Age is not a reason to quit life.

Shirley Allison

Hanging In

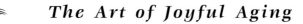

As I age I am more content to be with myself

And I know that I am my own best friend.

Paula Ridge

Friendship

When you get older it takes a lot longer

To do nothing.

Catherine Brandt

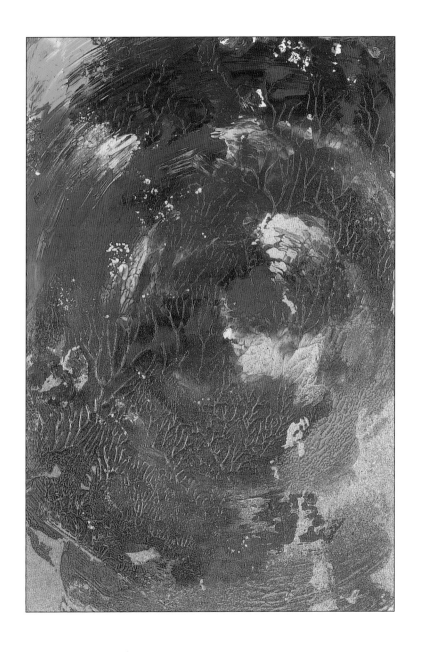

New Experience

It isn't the age in your life

It is the life in your age.

Abraham Lincoln

Insight

The joy of aging

Comes with realization

Of the wisdom we have

But have rarely used.

Alice Stowell

Slow Down

Reaching 50 was a celebration

Of where I have been,

What I have accomplished,

And who I have become,

A tribute to my self worth.

Marjorie Turner

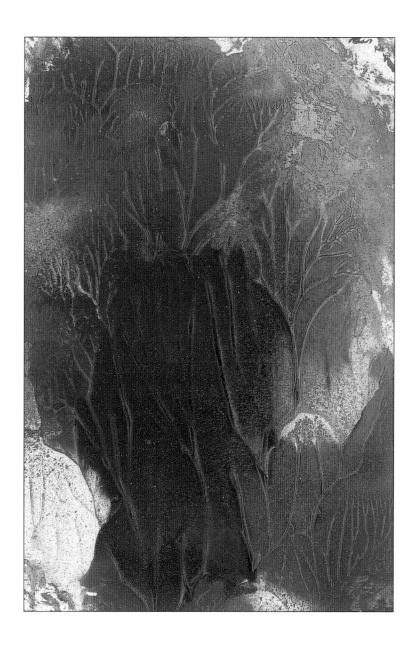

Self Worth

It has taken a long time to become young.

Pablo Picasso

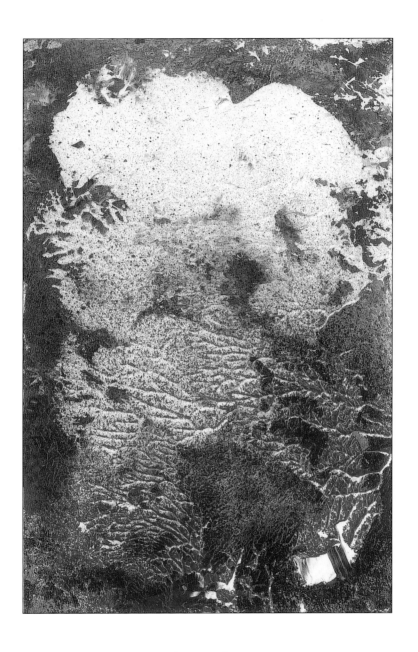

Timeless

Too much of a good thing

Can be wonderful.

Mae West

Wonder of Life

Aging is like the rainbow after the rain.

All the colors are there when you arrive

At maturity.

Jelko Yuresha

After the Rain

I will not make age an issue.

I am not going to exploit for political purposes

My opponent's youth and inexperience.

President Ronald Reagan,
*at age 73 at televised Presidential debate
with Walter Mondale October 2, 1984.*

Fall

The Issue

The best part of the art of living is to know

How to grow old gracefully.

Eric Hoffer
1902-1983

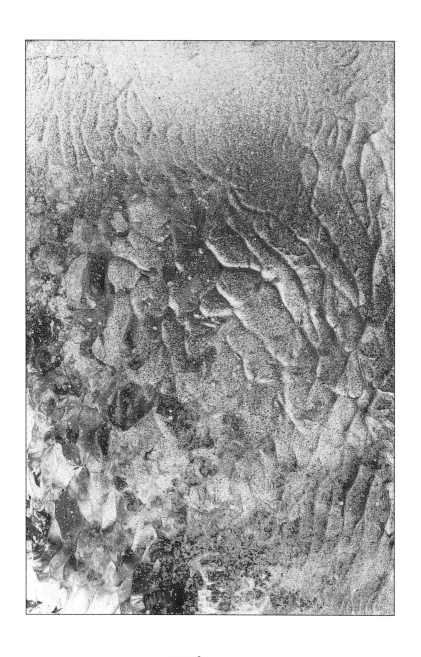

Winter

Aging is the realization of the riches of life,

Nature, friends, pets, children

And all the intangibles that are free.

Cyd Everett

Riches of Life

You remain young as long as you can

Still learn, accept new conventions and

Stand contradictions.

Marie Von Ebner Eschanbach
1830-1916

Eternal Youth

Wrinkles should merrily indicate

Where the smiles have been.

Mark Twain

W i n t e r

Smiles

Old or young we are all on our last cruise.

Robert Louis Stevenson

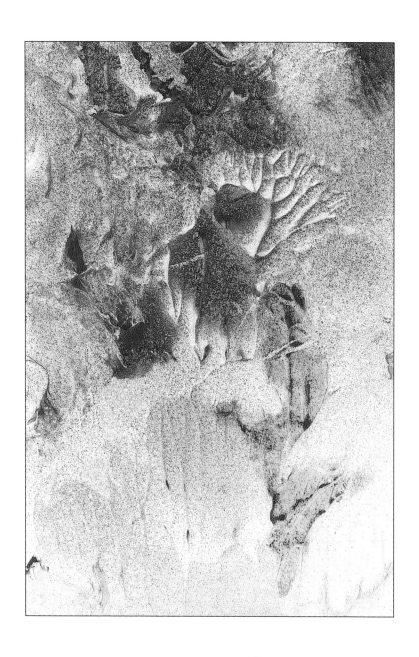

Last Cruise

I could not at any age, be content to

Take my place in a corner by the fireside

And simply look on.

Eleanor Roosevelt

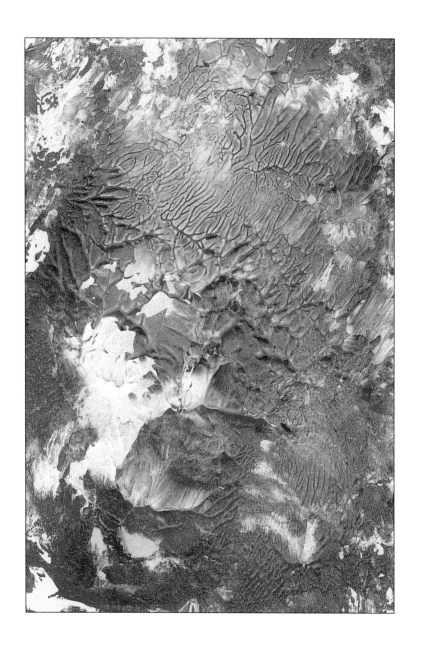

Moving Forward

Grab life by the tail and go for it.

Roz Yee

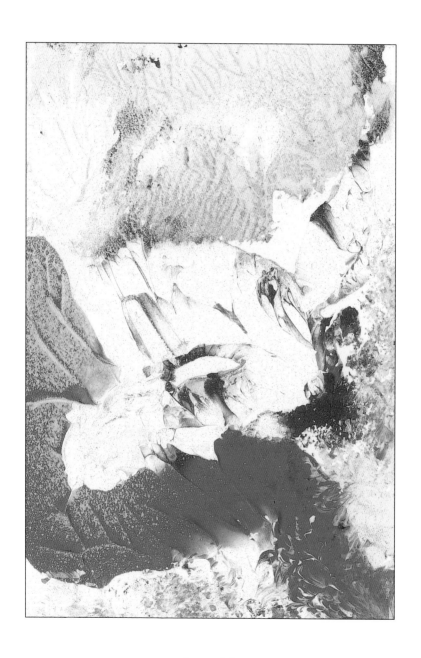

Vitality

Dear God,

Thank you for the day, its beauty and light.

Thank you for my chance to begin again.

Today, I am reborn, with peace,

Compassion, courage and wisdom.

Cathy Combs

A Prayer

You know you're getting old

When the candles cost more than the cake.

Bob Hope

Winter

Happy Birthday

Old age is like everything else,

To make a success of it,

You have to start young.

Fred Astaire

Love Life

If youth be a defect,

It is one that we outgrow too soon.

James Russell Lowell
1819-1891

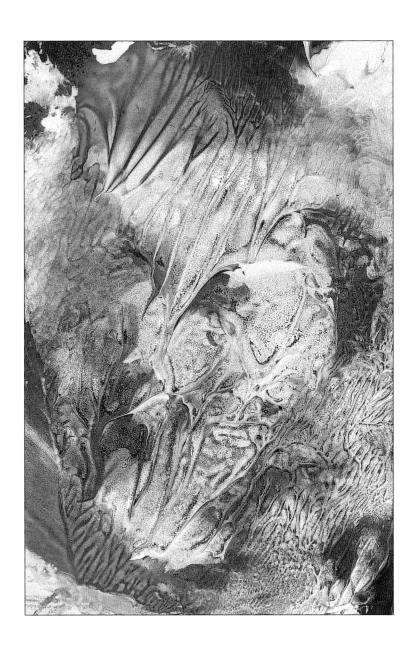

Harmony

Youth is not a time of life,

It is a state of mind.

General Douglas MacArthur

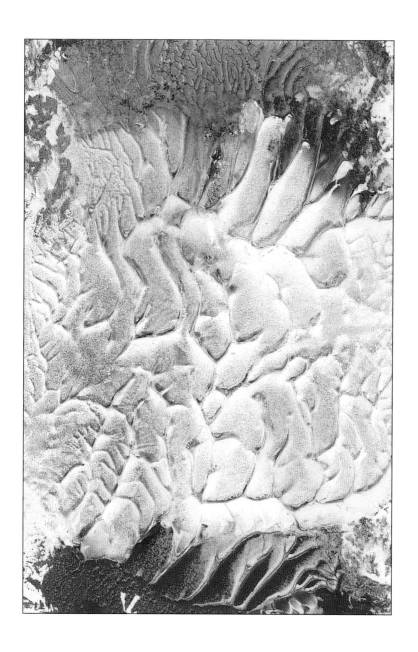

Mindfulness

What youth found outside,

The aging must find within...

Carl Jung
1875-1961

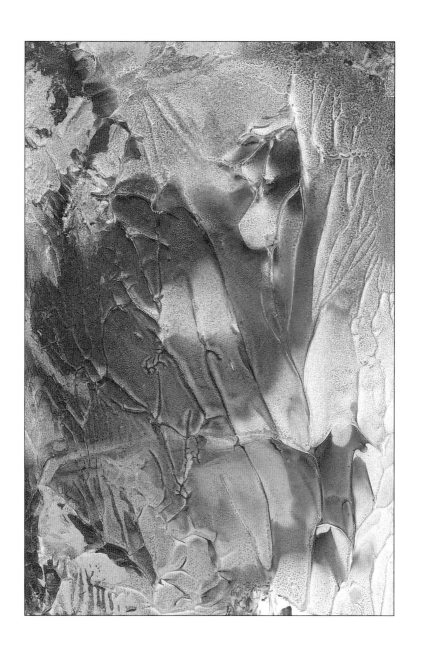

Within

With age I have learned never

To leave credit cards in my wallet

When traveling.

Carol Holmes

Insight

As one ages the simple things of life

Make one rich.

Benjamin Rike

Riches

When a woman ages, it is nice not to be

At the mercy of her hormones.

Cathy Biege

Surrender

When I got older I joined the I.R.S. Club.

I Remember Sex.

Helen Frankel

I.R.S. Club

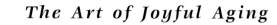

In youth we learn, with age we understand.

Marie Von Edner Eschenbach
1830-1916

Knowledge

Some people see aging as a dark tunnel,

Never seeing the light, whereas others

Embrace their age and life to the fullest.

As a Christian, I see life and aging

As a journey and gift,

Allowing us to grow closer to God.

Allyson Nicole Allison

Love

The secret of genius is to carry the spirit

Of the child into old age, which means

Never losing your enthusiasm.

Aldous Huxley

Youthfulness

IN SUMMATION
Have A Wonderful Life

To live an enjoyable life, *plan* it following principles that will bring you happiness, an approach that has provided success for others. Develop those traits that lead to a happy and healthy life. Select the right friends and the right life companion.

Follow a belief system. The National Geographical Society's "Great Religions of the World" examined Hinduism, Buddhism, Judaism, Islam and Christianity. Having studied all of the great religions adherents seem to have determined that it is the **Belief** that matters. Belief in a higher power and in the power of the subconscious mind brings you to a connection with the supreme being that affects the quality of your life.

Good health is most important in the enjoyment of life. Without good health it is difficult to enjoy many things. A good exercise program and consumption of the right type and amount of food helps to maintain health, appearance and attitude and enables a joyful later life. Avoiding or overcoming addiction to drugs or smoking and limiting alcohol consumption is essential. If you have an illness, seek competent medical attention. Overcoming life threatening illness requires appropriate medical treatment as well as a positive attitude and belief that you will.

Financial independence contributes strongly to enjoyment of life and especially when you are unable to produce income. Plan ahead and guard your assets.

Reduced responsibility as your parents pass on, and children become independent, provides freedom to choose your activities. Faith, good health and financial independence — all these factors contribute to your joy as you age. But even if these are denied, you still can enjoy living by maintaining a cheerful attitude and keeping the faith. The affirmations in this book will help you to do that and to maintain your sense of humor.

F. William Bauers, Jr.
Author

"Gaining and Maintaining Wealth"
"Where There's a Will ..."
"Memoirs of a Marauder Pilot"